> YoungW

Sense Poetry

Scotland & Wales

Edited By Tessa Mouat

25 Years of YoungWriters

First published in Great Britain in 2016 by:

YoungWriters

Coltsfoot Drive
Peterborough
PE2 9BF
Telephone: 01733 890066
Website: www.youngwriters.co.uk

All Rights Reserved
Book Design by Tim Christian
© Copyright Contributors 2016
SB ISBN 978-1-78624-423-9
Printed and bound in the UK by BookPrintingUK
Website: www.bookprintinguk.com
YB0281N

Foreword

Dear Reader,

Welcome to this book packed full of sights and smells, sounds and tastes!

Young Writers' Sense Poetry competition was specifically designed for Key Stage 1 children as a fun introduction to poetry and as a way to think about their senses: what the little poets can see, taste, smell, touch and hear in the world around them. Given the young age of the entrants, we endeavoured to include as many poems as possible. Here at Young Writers, we believe that seeing their work in print will inspire a love of reading and writing and give these young poets the confidence to develop their skills in the future. Poetry is a wonderful way to introduce young children to the idea of rhyme and rhythm and helps learning and development of communication, language and literacy skills.

With poems on a whole range of subjects from animals and everyday objects, through to emotions like love or hate, these young poets have used their creative writing abilities, sentence structure skills, thoughtful vocabulary and most importantly, their imaginations, to make their poems come alive. I hope you enjoy reading them as much as we have.

Tessa Mouat

Looks like you're in for a treat!

Contents

Winner:

Talibah Shah (7) - Coaltown Of Balgonie Primary School, Glenrothes   1

Auldhouse Primary School, East Kilbride

Emilee Jacqueline Leighton (6)	3
Flossie Hay (6)	4
Keiran MacDonald (6)	5

Coaltown Of Balgonie Primary School, Glenrothes

Cara Cairns (6)	6
Amy Emily Henderson (8)	7
Romea Pocock (7)	8
Miller Cunningham (6)	9
Claire Wight (6)	10
Alfie Meldrum (7)	11

Cwmfelinfach Primary School, Newport

Megan Cate Downes (7)	12
Eve Newnes (7)	14
Joshua Hurd (7)	16
Lucy-Jo Pawley (7)	17
Imogen Loren Simpkins (6)	18
Lewis Rawlings (6)	19
Eva Hardwick (7)	20
Rhianwen Rendall (7)	21

Liam Wallace (7)	22
Courtney Tweedy (6)	23
Liam Bromley (7)	24
Charlie Spicer (7)	25
Madison Evans (7)	26
Aaron Prudence (6)	27
Betsan Mai Barter (7)	28
Bailey Hughes (7)	29
Evan Maher (7)	30
Tori Alisha Woodham (7)	31
Jasmine Elizabeth Bayliss (7)	32
Charlie Mathieson (6)	33

Dunard Primary School, Glasgow

Sage Knight (6)	34
Brandon McGuigan (7)	35
Frankie Li (7)	36
Summer Delgado Davidson (6)	37
Keshia Burton (6)	38
Fiza Nasir (6)	39
Lewis Niven (7)	40
Lucie Louise Lelong-Byrne (6)	41
Calum David McInnes (7)	42
Shabnam Azam (6)	43
Sol Niven (7)	44
Darren Thomson (6)	45
Darius Cheskin (6)	46
Sophia Turner (6)	47
Neve Turpie (7)	48
Oliver Hall (6)	49

Alix Jane Anderson (7)	50
Tegan Sherlock (6)	51
Mio Greenland (6)	52
Eloia Pinho J Ribeiro (5)	53
Maomina Munsef (6)	54
Aiden Fitzpatrick (6)	55
Amber Sarah McGlynn (6)	56
Orin Hall (7)	57
Eva Forbes (6)	58
Abbie Doyle (6)	59
Jie Aron Goldie (6)	60
Sophie Totten (7)	61
Elysia Emily Laing (6)	62

Our Lady's RC Primary School, Stirling

Iwo Rutkowski (6)	63
Sienna Haris (5)	64
Kyle Nairns (5)	65
William Austin O'Malley Thompson (5)	66

Penygelli Primary School, Wrexham

Ruby Grace Whitfield (7)	67
Leon James Prince (6)	68
Samuel Lewis Armstrong (6)	69
Ellis McInerney (6)	70
Sophie Arthur (6)	71
Zack Jones (6)	72
Nieve Dillon (7)	73
Ella Grace Clorley-Jones (7)	74
Miriam Caitlin Rumsey (6)	75
Matthew Keats (6)	76
Rhys David Ineson (6)	77
Barbara Kokeny (7)	78

Maddison Savannah-Rose Harrison (7)	79
Lily Isabella Beech (6)	80
Skyler Jones (6)	81
Tegan Casey Williams (6)	82
Harriet Roberts (6)	83
Imogen Wright (5)	84

Portsoy Primary School, Banff

Peyton Runcie (6)	85
Laura Sophie McManus (6)	86
Lyla Rose Booth (6)	87
Rhys Henderson (7)	88
Bella Mathieson (6)	89
Olly McKenzie (6)	90
Madison Taylor (7)	91
R-Jay Robertson (7)	92
Oliver Merson (5)	93
Aidan Clark (6)	94
Kenzi Gauld (6)	95
Mason John Taylor (7)	96
Sienna Louise Angus (6)	97
Ruby Rose Wilson (6)	98
Alesha Wishart-Turner (6)	99

Presteigne Primary School, Presteigne

Alfie David Goodwin (7)	100
Mair Thomas (6)	101
John Andre Rodrigues-Nutting (7)	102
Benjamin Williams (7)	103
Ferdi Özsoylu (6)	104
Chloe Lloyd-Bithell (7)	105
Darcy Barden (7)	106
Hunter Jones (6)	107
Finley James Williams (6)	108
Katie Mae Williams (6)	109

Rhys Morgan (7) 110
Max Scott (6) 111
Josie Simcock (7) 112

St Charles Primary School, Glasgow

Lauren Martin (7) 113
Ruby Cosh 114
Luke Bierey (7) 115
Ellie Joanna Joanna Drysdale (5) 116
Ayat Amin (7) 117
Cerys Anne Newman (7) 118
Charley Helen McEwan (7) 119
Jack James McGonigle (7) 120
Aliex Murray (7) 121
Beth Wilson (7) 122
Emily Tollett (7) 123
Ayaan Azam (6) 124
Grace Olivia Anderson (5) 125
Shay Farquhar (5) 126
Olivia Teresa Dougan-Wark 127
Lewis Hamilton (5) 128
Daniel McGhee (5) 129
Olivia Grace Bradley (5) 130
Ryan James O'Hara (5) 131
Rayyan Amin (5) 132
Charlotte Kelly (6) 133
Taylor Bokas (5) 134
Shay Arkinson (5) 135
Brody Boyd (5) 136
Connor Craig (5) 137
Abigail Kirkland (6) 138
Keira Faith McDonald (6) 139
Katrine Friel (7) 140

Straiton Primary School, Maybole

Lily May (5) 141

The Poems

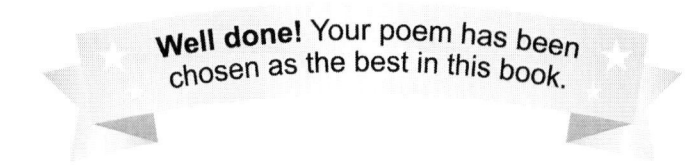

Well done! Your poem has been chosen as the best in this book.

Seaside Senses Poem

I could hear the magical waves
Splashing up and down
It sounded like a mystery
I couldn't stop listening
To the dangerous deep blue sea

I could touch the beautiful cold sea
It made me dream
Which is why it is called the magical waves

I could taste some delicious eye-catching
Tasty bubblegum ice cream
It was very cold

I could smell disgusting stargazer fish in the sea
If I saw it in my dreams I would've screamed

I could see the famous boat, the Titanic
Everybody at the seaside stood still,
Frozen and astonished
After an hour everybody started to scream,
Saying, 'It's the Titanic!'

Talibah Shah (7)
Coaltown Of Balgonie Primary School, Glenrothes

The Seaside

I can see the beautiful, golden, smiling sun.
I can hear the waves crashing
Into the golden, sparkling sand.
I can smell the yummy fish
Cooking on the barbecue.
I can feel the lovely soft sand.
I can taste the sweet strawberry ice cream
And it was really, really yummy.

Emilee Jacqueline Leighton (6)
Auldhouse Primary School, East Kilbride

Bulgaria's Beach

I can see the beautiful golden sun.
I can hear the waves crashing
On the golden beach.
I can smell ice cream and ice lollies.
I can feel the seaweed, it is slimy.
I can taste the strawberry ice cream,
It is really tasty.

Flossie Hay (6)
Auldhouse Primary School, East Kilbride

My Seaside Poem

I can see the lovely sun.
I can hear children playing.
I can smell vanilla ice cream.
I can feel the seashells.
I can taste cheese sandwiches, they are yummy.

Keiran MacDonald (6)
Auldhouse Primary School, East Kilbride

Seaside Senses Poem

At the coast,
I hear the splashing waves
rubbing against the rocks
It splashes so loudly it gives me a shock

At the coast,
I feel the hard seashells with sea creatures inside
They surface because of the tide

At the coast,
I see the seagulls flying across the sky
They have white feathers and I don't know why

At the coast,
I can smell the salty sea water and the fresh breeze
It is so windy it blows the trees

At the coast,
I taste the cold vanilla ice cream and it's so yummy
It tickles my tummy!

Cara Cairns (6)
Coaltown Of Balgonie Primary School, Glenrothes

Seaside Senses Poem

At the seaside,
I can hear the swooshing seabed crack!
It all goes quiet and I jump back
'Argh!' I gasp, shocked

At the seaside,
I can touch the crackling sand in my hand

At the seaside,
I can see dolphins paddle out to sea
'Wow!' I say

At the seaside,
I can taste the salty sea in my mouth
I want it, I think

At the seaside,
I can smell the sweet sausages sizzling away.

Amy Emily Henderson (8)
Coaltown Of Balgonie Primary School, Glenrothes

Seaside Senses Poem

At the seaside,
I smell some smoky bonfire
It's like red-hot fire

When I go to the seaside,
I taste coconut water which tastes good to me!

At the seaside,
I hear people diving in the ocean
It's just like a magic potion

At the seaside,
I can see boats far away at sea
It's like a shaking tree

I feel cold yucky fish, like sushi.

Romea Pocock (7)
Coaltown Of Balgonie Primary School, Glenrothes

Seaside Senses Poem

At the rock pool,
I could see the sparkling sea
I could see the tide and fog

At the rock pool,
I could hear my chocolate bar
I could hear crabs spin
Like a shark snapping its jaw

At the rock pool,
The waves splashed like a spaceship landing

At the rock pool,
I could touch the burning sand
I made a sandcastle.

Miller Cunningham (6)
Coaltown Of Balgonie Primary School, Glenrothes

Seaside Senses Poem

When I go to the seaside,
I can hear the waves going up and down
I can touch the hot sand burning my toes
I can see the red crabs and lobsters,
The umbrellas and sunbeds
I can smell chicken cooking in a kitchen
I can taste nice fruity ice cream and cakes
That are freshly baked
It's so nice to be at the seaside!
The day ends, the sun sets, the sea goes to bed.

Claire Wight (6)
Coaltown Of Balgonie Primary School, Glenrothes

Seaside Senses Poem

I can hear my friends at the beach
I can touch the water
I can smell sausages
I can see the beach
I can taste chocolate.

Alfie Meldrum (7)
Coaltown Of Balgonie Primary School, Glenrothes

Senses At The Funfair

I can hear loud laughter, because the rides zooooooom so fast,
I can hear roller coasters clatter as the people fly past,
I can hear rock-star music, and bumping bumper cars,
All the sounds go travelling up to the night stars.

I have sticky fingers from eating sugary treats,
I feel the squashy bouncy castle under my feet,
I want to touch the water from the game called hook-a-duck,
I hope I win a prize! Wish me luck!

I can smell the grass in-between my tippy-toes,
Smells of sausages and lollipops drift up my nose,
I can smell the flowers as the butterflies fly by,
I can smell the seaside and the fresh summer sky.

I can taste burgers and popcorn and sweets,
I imagine I can taste everything I want to eat!
I can taste doughnuts and candyfloss and pop,
I can taste so much my tummy might pop!

I can see flashing lights everywhere,
On rides, on roller coasters, all over the fair,
I can see people and games and shops,
I can see, hear, taste, touch and smell lots and lots.

Megan Cate Downes (7)
Cwmfelinfach Primary School, Newport

Seasons

In summer I love the smell of fresh cut grass,
The sight of butterflies flying past.
The touch of warmth from the sun,
The taste of strawberries freshly done
And hearing the sounds of summer fun.

In autumn I love the smell of apple pie,
The prickly conkers fallen from the sky.
The taste of sweets on Halloween,
The sound of fireworks makes me beam
And the sight of the autumn leaves.

In winter I love the taste of yummy Christmas lunch,
The sight of presents in a bunch.
The sound of carol singers at the door,
The touch of wrapping paper being torn
And the smell of a long fire
Where I'm sure to be warm.

In spring I love seeing the new green leaves
In the trees,
Hearing the birds singing happily.
The smell of daffodils on the farm,
Touching the Easter egg wrapped to charm
And tasting my favourite treat:
Chocolate eggs so sweet!

Eve Newnes (7)
Cwmfelinfach Primary School, Newport

George

George was my friend but in the end he died,
I was very sad and a little bit mad.
I remember that his back was smooth
But he couldn't move very fast.
I remember him barking with joy
Then Grandma saying, 'Oi!'
Grandad was cross
But George didn't mind because he was the boss.
He was very hairy
Some people thought he was very scary.
He smelt like flowers
He played for hours.
He was running, chasing birds and cats
And knocked over all the hats.
He loved digging bones
And stealing ice cream cones
George the dog was a lovely dog
I miss him every day
And I will always remember him.

Joshua Hurd (7)
Cwmfelinfach Primary School, Newport

Fun At The Fair

The sun is shining
I can feel the heat
As I sit on the beach so I can eat
The tastiest ice cream as my treat
The music's loud, the lights are bright
The pier looks so nice at night
The children scream as they go past
On the rides that are so fast
'It's my turn next!' I'll hold on tight
As I don't want a fright
The smell of doughnuts fills the air
I don't want any I feel sick from the fair.

Lucy-Jo Pawley (7)
Cwmfelinfach Primary School, Newport

The Funfair

I love going to the funfair
The burgers, candyfloss and popcorn
All smell yummy and sweet
Going on the rides makes me feel very excited
The taste of the freezing cold ice cream
Makes me shiver inside
I can touch fluffy clouds
When I'm on the big roller coaster
I can hear lots of noise
When people are on the fast rides
Seeing everybody enjoying themselves
Makes me very happy.

Imogen Loren Simpkins (6)
Cwmfelinfach Primary School, Newport

Candyfloss

Standing eating candyfloss
Watching the rides go round
With beautiful lights and sound

Standing eating candyfloss
The twister goes in and out
All the children scream and shout

Standing eating candyfloss
A smell goes passing through
Just around the corner
There are doughnuts waiting for you.

Lewis Rawlings (6)
Cwmfelinfach Primary School, Newport

Senses At The Funfair

Fresh doughnuts,
The smell fills the air under the starlit sky,
Nothing like hearing the screams
And laughing of people on the rides.
Feeling the fluffy candyfloss
And a slurp of ice-cold drinks,
And seeing all the pretty lights and smiley faces,
It's a wonderful place to be,
Really exciting things to taste
Like gooey marshmallows
And hot chocolate to keep us warm at the fair.

Eva Hardwick (7)
Cwmfelinfach Primary School, Newport

Fantastic Fireworks

Whee! Look at that one
So colourful and bright
Straight up high
In the sky
Through the darkness of the night.

Bang! Whoosh! They are so loud,
Straight, twisty into the cloud
Red, yellow, pink and blue
Children holding sparklers
And the adults too.

Rhianwen Rendall (7)
Cwmfelinfach Primary School, Newport

Day At The Beach

One day I went to the beach
To see what I could see,
I saw a seagull as white as could be.
I had a ride on a donkey, he was a fine steed,
I found a crab with big claws under the seaweed.
I liked the water on my toes
And the smell of the sea up my nose.
I ate candyfloss with my spare hand.
When I got home, in my pocket,
I found lots of sand.

Liam Wallace (7)
Cwmfelinfach Primary School, Newport

Funfair

I went to the fair
I tasted hard, tasty sweets and I saw fast, big rides
Then I heard lovely music
After, I touched cold bars
Last, I smelt lovely, cold fresh air
The bright glowing lights showed me where my family was
With a token I can go on a ride
I can hear screaming voices
I can always eat hot hot dogs.
I can smell yummy burgers.

Courtney Tweedy (6)
Cwmfelinfach Primary School, Newport

Funfair

Win a teddy, throw a dart,
The roller coaster is about to start.
People laughing, screaming too,
People waiting in a queue.
Fluffy candyfloss on a stick
Hot dogs or doughnuts, take your pick.
On the big wheel up so high
I feel like I can touch the sky.
The funfair has come to an end
I can't wait to go home and tell my friends.

Liam Bromley (7)
Cwmfelinfach Primary School, Newport

Moon Cheese

Everyone knows the moon's made of cheese,
The countdown's begun and I feel a bit nervous
My seatbelt is tight and the engines are roaring
We are off into space, the rocket's soaring
We land on the moon and the moon rocks feel dusty in the cool moon breeze
Lunchtime is here, time for moon cheese
I like mine warm with mushy peas
It might taste great, it might be alright
As day soon quickly turns into night.

Charlie Spicer (7)
Cwmfelinfach Primary School, Newport

The Beach

The beach makes me happy, I can see the sea,
Donkey rides and happy smiles,
'Take a picture of me!'
Sun, sea and sandcastles, it's the life for me,
I've been coming to the beach since I was three!
The sun is hot, the sky is blue
Ice creams are melting too.
Down to the sea I go, one, two, three,
'Catch me if you can!' I shout. It's the life for me.

Madison Evans (7)
Cwmfelinfach Primary School, Newport

I Went To The Fair

I went to the fair
And all I did was stare
At all the rides that were there
I found the merry-go-round
And followed it as it went round
I saw the roller coaster
And got a bit closer
It went up and down
And my belly turned upside down.

Aaron Prudence (6)
Cwmfelinfach Primary School, Newport

Gymnastics

I felt the wooden floor on my feet
and the hard beam,
I heard Coach's voice talking when I was looking
at the apparatus,
blue mats everywhere.
I could smell the chalk and blue mats after running,
jumping, climbing over beams.
I could feel and hear my heart beating
That cold water tasted great.

Betsan Mai Barter (7)
Cwmfelinfach Primary School, Newport

Fun At The Fair

People laughing all around,
Having fun at the fairground.
Lots of lights like flashing stars,
Zooming past in bumper cars.
Yummy food and sweets all bright,
Everything around is a wonderful sight!
There's loads of things for you to see,
When you're at the fairground with your family.

Bailey Hughes (7)
Cwmfelinfach Primary School, Newport

Fun At The Fair

Ice cream yummy, drinks bubbly
Sweets swirling in my tummy
I jump on rides, lights flashing, music playing
Whizzing, whirling, spinning, twirling
Excitement in the air
People smiling, laughing, shouting
They all love the colourful fair.

Evan Maher (7)
Cwmfelinfach Primary School, Newport

Funfair

F amilies
U nhappy parents
N agging
F alling
A nd
I love
R ides.

Tori Alisha Woodham (7)
Cwmfelinfach Primary School, Newport

A Poem About A Poem

I can touch the pencil that is writing my poem,
I can smell the rubber rubbing out my words,
I can see the words about my poem,
I can taste what I am writing,
I can taste ice cream in a poem about ice cream,
I can hear the music in what I am writing.

Jasmine Elizabeth Bayliss (7)
Cwmfelinfach Primary School, Newport

Nature Senses

I can smell the salty sea,
I can touch the spiky grass,
I can hear the happy crickets,
I can see the chirpy birds,
I can taste the minty leaves,
I love nature.

Charlie Mathieson (6)
Cwmfelinfach Primary School, Newport

I Sense The Jungle

As I walk in the jungle,
I can feel the grass tickling my feet...
I can taste sweet honey as I climb a tall tree...
I can see a stripy tiger...
I can hear the chattering monkeys...
I can smell the lovely blooming flowers.

Sage Knight (6)
Dunard Primary School, Glasgow

My Minecraft Poem

I can see green Creepers
I can touch black Endermen
I can see Mobs
I can smell pork chops cooking in a furnace
I can see my house and dog
I see a strange man mining for diamonds and coal
He looks at me
When I see his eyes they are all white
I run so fast I cannot see him
Then he traps me in a cage.

Brandon McGuigan (7)
Dunard Primary School, Glasgow

In My Box

Inspired by 'Magic Box' by Kit Wright

In my box I will put...
the smell of a large delicious pizza.
It's got cheese, chicken and popcorn and it's just
got delivered.
In my box I will put...
the taste of a delicious ice cream.
It's got three flavours, chocolate, strawberry
and vanilla.
In my box I will put...
the feel of a green shiny book.
Inside will be funny stories.
In my box I will put...
the sight of a very big rainbow with lots of colours.
In my box I will put...
the sound of a bell ringing.
It means home time.

Frankie Li (7)
Dunard Primary School, Glasgow

The Lovely Nutella

The Nutella, oh what a wonderful thing
It is all that nutty flavour and creamy flavour as well
The chocolatey flavour is my favourite
Oh and the smell, that wonderful smell
That yummy smell running up my nose
It looks like a bowl of brown cream and that makes it look great.

Summer Delgado Davidson (6)
Dunard Primary School, Glasgow

I Like Pizza

I love pizza, it's yummy
Pizza is nice
The cheese is stringy and chewy
It smells so yummy
It tastes nice and hot in my mouth
It smells and tastes stringy.

Keshia Burton (6)
Dunard Primary School, Glasgow

Untitled

Strawberry ice cream is yummy
I love it in my tummy
Strawberry ice cream is pink
It is delicious
I think the strawberry ice cream tastes scrumptious
and strawberry ice cream is my favourite.

Fiza Nasir (6)
Dunard Primary School, Glasgow

Untitled

You can touch the seats and the tickets and the popcorn and the doors
And you can taste the popcorn and sweets
And you can hear the babies crying and the people laughing at the funny bits
And I can hear the drinks going *sluuuuuuuurp!*
And hear the popcorn crunching and the doors closing.

Lewis Niven (7)
Dunard Primary School, Glasgow

Wind And The Woods

As I run within the breeze
I feel the wind in my hair
And when I hear the wind, I think of birds singing
When I get cold I reach into my bag and I pull out a flask of hot chocolate
And when I look around I feel so happy because I am around nature.

Lucie Louise Lelong-Byrne (6)
Dunard Primary School, Glasgow

Spring

Spring feels like chocolate

Spring tastes like strawberry ice cream

Spring smells like daffodils

Spring feels like cold and rain and flowers

Spring smells like sweets and bubblegum and trees.

Calum David McInnes (7)
Dunard Primary School, Glasgow

Bubbles

Bubblegum smells nice and sweet
I never drop it in the street
Bubblegum tastes like strawberry
Bubblegum sounds like a loud pop
Bubblegum looks like blue and pink balloons.

Shabnam Azam (6)
Dunard Primary School, Glasgow

Untitled

I love the swing park
I have to go home when it's dark
I love to play on the swings
It is one of my favourite things to do
I fly down the long chute.

Sol Niven (7)
Dunard Primary School, Glasgow

Yummy In My Tummy

Chocolate cake tastes yummy in my tummy
and the chocolate on the top tastes like chocolate apple
And the sponge reminds me of my favourite
real sponge
And chocolate cake feels slimy and squishy
It smells like melted chocolate.

Darren Thomson (6)
Dunard Primary School, Glasgow

Dinosaurs

Dinosaurs smell like yucky bones and stinky skin
Dinosaurs taste like yucky bones and a
squelchy tongue
Dinosaurs feel like yucky bones and looking eyes and stinky skin and little arms and smooth teeth
Dinosaurs look like a tail and a skull and yucky bones and mostly a thief.

Darius Cheskin (6)
Dunard Primary School, Glasgow

As I Walk Through The Jungle

As I walk through the jungle,
I can feel the branches tickling me.
As I jog through the jungle,
I can taste juicy mangoes.
As I run through the jungle,
I can see a furry tiger.
As I run through the jungle,
I can hear the wind brushing the leaves.
As I walk through the jungle,
I can smell the hot air.

Sophia Turner (6)
Dunard Primary School, Glasgow

Buddy

Buddy, Buddy when in puddles smells like wet dog
And just out of the puddles he smells and looks like a dirty dog
He makes a lot of noise barking, growling and playing tug of war
He is very fluffy and warm on my skin.

Neve Turpie (7)
Dunard Primary School, Glasgow

Untitled

When I touch bubblegum it feels like balloons in my mouth
It smells like cola
It sounds like a loud pop in my ear
It looks like a gigantic football coming out of my mouth.

Oliver Hall (6)
Dunard Primary School, Glasgow

Ice Cream

Inspired by 'Magic Box' by Kit Wright

In my box I will put,
the taste of ice cream and the biggest ice cream ever.
In my box I will put,
the smell of mint chocolate and it will be cold but
very yummy.
It is white mint chocolate, ready to eat.
In my box I will put,
some sunshine, ready to shine when it is opened up.
It will shine onto my colourful ice cream but hopefully it
won't melt it.

Alix Jane Anderson (7)
Dunard Primary School, Glasgow

In My Box

Inspired by 'Magic Box' by Kit Wright

In my box I will put a toffee cake
with a strawberry on top.
In my box I will put a strawberry milkshake
with marshmallows and strawberries.
In my box I will put a kitten so I can pet it.
In my box I will put some flowers
because they smell lovely.
In my box I will put some friends
so they can sing to me.

Tegan Sherlock (6)
Dunard Primary School, Glasgow

I Am Going To The Rainforest

As I walk through the rainforest,
I can feel the smooth air blowing.
As I run down the rainforest,
I can taste the tropical fruit.
As I skip into the rainforest,
I can see a flock of birds.
As I hop deep into the rainforest,
I can hear the trees and bushes rustling.

Mio Greenland (6)
Dunard Primary School, Glasgow

As I Walk Through The Jungle

As I walk through the jungle,
I can see the green plants.
As I hop through the jungle,
I can taste the lovely fruit.
As I run through the jungle,
I can feel the spiky plants.
As I sneak through the jungle,
I can smell the yucky mud!

Eloia Pinho J Ribeiro (5)
Dunard Primary School, Glasgow

In My Dream

I saw a queen
She heard a bee
Buzzing around her feet
She sang a song
And flowers danced
She held a sparrow
Up in the sky.

Maomina Munsef (6)
Dunard Primary School, Glasgow

Untitled

In spring it smells like flowers and bubblegum
It tastes like strawberries
I can see baby animals, lambs and chickens.

Aiden Fitzpatrick (6)
Dunard Primary School, Glasgow

The Jungle

As I walk in the jungle,
I can feel the water dripping onto me.
I can see the pineapples dripping onto me.
I can smell the droppings from the animals.
I can see elephants stomping their feet.
I can hear birds chirping.

Amber Sarah McGlynn (6)
Dunard Primary School, Glasgow

In My Box
Inspired by 'Magic Box' by Kit Wright

In my box I will put...
the smell of my chocolate bunny.
I will put the feel of our pet hamsters
and I will put in the sight of my birthday cake.
In my box I will put...
the taste of pizza and chocolate.

Orin Hall (7)
Dunard Primary School, Glasgow

Walking Through The Jungle

As I skip through the jungle,
I can feel coconuts bouncing off my head.
I can taste the sweet and juicy mangoes.
I can see the toucan.
I can hear the bees buzzing loudly.
I can smell the tropical flowers.

Eva Forbes (6)
Dunard Primary School, Glasgow

Smelly Socks

Inspired by 'Magic Box' by Kit Wright

In my box there are lots of socks,
The gooey, smelly, cheesy type
Some have lots of dots and stripes.

The box is soft, small and there's a click,
The smell would make you really sick.

Abbie Doyle (6)
Dunard Primary School, Glasgow

Yucky Poo

As I walk in the jungle,
I can feel the honey dripping on my head.
I can taste juicy strawberries.
I can see enormous elephants.
I can hear chattering monkeys.
I can smell yucky poo!

Jie Aron Goldie (6)
Dunard Primary School, Glasgow

The Magic Box

Inspired by 'Magic Box' by Kit Wright

In my box I will place
The blue, blue ocean
And the gas of a rocket,
The sound of a tree,
The taste of white chocolate
And the smell of freshly made ice cream.

Sophie Totten (7)
Dunard Primary School, Glasgow

Sunny Beach

I run on the beach,
Sand wet beneath my feet.
I hear the waves,
I smell the sea,
Will you have ice cream with me?
Let's enjoy the sun.

Elysia Emily Laing (6)
Dunard Primary School, Glasgow

Untitled

Chocolate smells minty like fresh leaves on a tree.
Chocolate looks shiny like stars in the sky.
Chocolate feels cold like ice on a winter's day.
Chocolate sounds like popping popcorn.
Chocolate tastes rich like dry cocoa.

Iwo Rutkowski (6)
Our Lady's RC Primary School, Stirling

Chocolate

Chocolate smells minty like fresh minty toothpaste.
Chocolate looks dark like the night sky.
Chocolate feels hard like my writing table.
Chocolate sounds like cracking glass.
Chocolate tastes strong like hot coffee.

Sienna Haris (5)
Our Lady's RC Primary School, Stirling

Mmm... Yum

Chocolate smells as minty as mouthwash.
Chocolate looks brown like soft, wet mud.
Chocolate feels thin like plywood.
Chocolate sounds like cracking crackers.
Chocolate tastes like home-made ice cream.

Kyle Nairns (5)
Our Lady's RC Primary School, Stirling

Untitled

Chocolate smells like my mum's beautiful perfume.
Chocolate looks brown like a big, scruffy dog.
Chocolate feels hard like a brick chimney.
Chocolate sounds like snapping teeth.

William Austin O'Malley Thompson (5)
Our Lady's RC Primary School, Stirling

Bonfire Night

I can hear fireworks explode.
I can hear people laughing.
I can hear bombs exploding.

I can taste squashy marshmallows.
I can taste yummy beans.
I can taste skinny hot dogs.

I can touch smooth marshmallows.
I can touch hard sparkler sticks.
I can touch soft gloves.

I can see crackling sparklers.
I can see booming fireworks.

I can smell hot smoke.

Ruby Grace Whitfield (7)
Penygelli Primary School, Wrexham

My Days At School

In school I see Miss Griffiths and she rules.
In school I see children working.
In school I can smell satsumas.
In school I can taste chicken curry at dinner time.
In school I touch my snake.
In school I can hear children screaming in the yard,
I see the boys playing football.
In school I smell fresh air.
In school I touch the table.
In school I taste roast dinner.
In school I hear wind outside.
In school I can see my work on the wall.
In school I see teachers.

Leon James Prince (6)
Penygelli Primary School, Wrexham

My Senses

In school I can see Miss Griffiths.
I can see blocks falling on the floor.
I can smell air.
I can taste my dinner.
I can hear noise.
I can touch the books.
I can see people.
I can see school.
I can smell pizza.
I can hear birds.
I can feel the pen.
I can see different classes.

Samuel Lewis Armstrong (6)
Penygelli Primary School, Wrexham

Untitled

In school I can see Mrs Griffiths,
she is doing cutting.
In school I can smell Mrs Griffiths' perfume.
In school I can smell food.
In school I can touch the books.
In school I can touch the ground
when I am playing on the grass.
In school I can touch the table.
In school I can feel the walls.
In school I can feel my books.

Ellis McInerney (6)
Penygelli Primary School, Wrexham

My Senses At School

In school I can see Miss Griffiths.
In school I can see house points.
In school I can taste chicken.
In school I can taste pizza.
In school I can feel chairs.
In school I can feel the pirate ship.
In school I can smell curry.
In school I can smell Play-Doh.
In school I can hear screaming.
In school I can hear people.

Sophie Arthur (6)
Penygelli Primary School, Wrexham

Zack's Senses

I can see the teachers in school because they rule.
I can see the board on the wall,
In PE I play with a ball.
At lunch I taste a chicken dinner and it's a winner.
I taste satsumas at snack and my name is Zack.
I can touch a log because I'm a log.
I can touch the blocks in my socks.
I can smell dinner because it's a winner.
I can smell chocolate and it looks scrumptious.

Zack Jones (6)
Penygelli Primary School, Wrexham

Summer

In summer I can taste very cold ice cream,
I can drink cold fizzy drinks,
I can smell sweet-smelling flowers
And hot barbecues,
I can see people relaxing in their hot gardens
And noisy children playing outside,
I feel very hot and it feels very relaxing,
I can hear the loud tweeting birds
And the loud ice cream van.

Nieve Dillon (7)
Penygelli Primary School, Wrexham

Bonfire Night

I can taste soft chips and brown hot dogs.
I can hear a bonfire and fireworks.
I can taste squishy marshmallows.
I can taste lovely beans.
I can touch hard glowsticks.
I can smell hot fire and yummy doughnuts.
I can touch smooth marshmallows.
I can taste chocolate sticks.
I can hear the fireworks go *bang!*

Ella Grace Clorley-Jones (7)
Penygelli Primary School, Wrexham

In School

In school I can see Miss Griffiths working with us on the table.
In school I can see and smell fruit that is tasty and yummy and I'm hungry.
In school I can touch my snack which is an apple and I do a bit of a rapple.
In school I can hear the sound of running as we play.
In school I can see my piece of paper.

Miriam Caitlin Rumsey (6)
Penygelli Primary School, Wrexham

Christmas

I can taste nice dinner and pudding,
I can hear noisy crackers and nice songs and wrapping paper,
I can smell yummy dinner,
I can see Santa and a tree and family and food,
I can touch wrapping paper and presents and a tree and decorations.

Matthew Keats (6)
Penygelli Primary School, Wrexham

Happiness

Happiness sounds like loud cheery laughing.
Happiness tastes like juicy apples and sweet oranges.
Happiness smells like beautiful flowers.
Happiness looks like smiley faces.
Happiness feels like happy breezes and
beautiful flowers.

Rhys David Ineson (6)
Penygelli Primary School, Wrexham

Birthdays

I can taste chocolate cake and cold ice cream.
I can hear my sister singing
And my mum is laughing.
I can touch red presents and funny toys.
I can see you smiling and cool cakes.
I can smell hot candles and lovely foods.

Barbara Kokeny (7)
Penygelli Primary School, Wrexham

Autumn

In autumn I can see the leaves swaying in the air,
In autumn I can smell burning fireworks in the air,
In autumn I can taste sweet Halloween treats,
In autumn I can hear big trees blowing in the wind,
In autumn I can feel crunchy leaves under my feet.

Maddison Savannah-Rose Harrison (7)
Penygelli Primary School, Wrexham

Summer

In summer I can hear buzzing bees,
In summer I can smell smoky barbecues,
In summer I can taste vanilla ice cream,
In summer I can see beautiful flowers,
In summer I can touch newborn chicks.

Lily Isabella Beech (6)
Penygelli Primary School, Wrexham

Spring

In spring I can taste chocolate eggs,
In spring I can hear the ice cream van,
In spring I can touch flowers and pretty chicks,
In spring I can see baby lambs,
In spring I can smell cut grass.

Skyler Jones (6)
Penygelli Primary School, Wrexham

Halloween

I have sticky lollies and marshmallows,
I can hear screaming and footsteps,
I can touch a smooth, round pumpkin,
I can smell pumpkins being lit up,
I can see dinner cooking.

Tegan Casey Williams (6)
Penygelli Primary School, Wrexham

I Can...

I can smell fresh air from outside.
I can taste our snack.
I can feel Braille when Mrs Walley lets me.
I can hear the wood
When the people are banging on the table.

Harriet Roberts (6)
Penygelli Primary School, Wrexham

Lemonade

I can taste the bitter lemons,
I can smell lemon juice,
I can see the bubbles rising,
I can touch fizzy bubbles,
I can hear bubbles popping.

Imogen Wright (5)
Penygelli Primary School, Wrexham

Minibeasts

I can see a butterfly.
I can taste honey.
I can feel an ant walking on my hand.
I can smell honey in a beehive.
I can hear buzzing in the trees.
I see bees buzzing in the beehive.
I can feel a snail slithering on my hand.
I can see a ladybird flying.
I can hear a grasshopper hopping in the grass.
I can see a slug in the garden.
I can feel a butterfly in my hand.
I can see a ladybird.
I can feel a caterpillar.

Peyton Runcie (6)
Portsoy Primary School, Banff

Minibeasts

I can smell bees collecting honey.
I can hear crickets chirruping on the leaves.
I can see beetles crawling up my hand.
I can hear a butterfly's wings fluttering.
I can see a spiderweb in the garden.
I can hear a bee buzzing around me.
I can touch the smooth beetles.
I can see a beautiful butterfly.
I can hear a caterpillar scuttling on the leaves.
I can feel the bumpy bugs.

Laura Sophie McManus (6)
Portsoy Primary School, Banff

Minibeasts

I can see a spiderweb with dew on it.
I can feel a slimy snail.
I can taste sticky, sweet, golden honey.
I can smell a worm in compost.
I can hear a bee buzzing in a treetop.
I love to see a butterfly in the sky with its beautiful wings in the sunlight.
I can also see a beehive with honey going out of it.
I touched a slimy snail and I picked it up.
I love to hear caterpillars munching the leaves.

Lyla Rose Booth (6)
Portsoy Primary School, Banff

Minibeasts

I can see a beehive,
Under the hive there are loads of snails.
I can see a ladybug crawling up my arm.
I can taste a snail and it is gross.
I can feel a butterfly on my hand.
I can smell grass in someone's garden.
I can hear a cricket, it is a loud sound
It's coming from that house
Where the person is cutting the grass.

Rhys Henderson (7)
Portsoy Primary School, Banff

Minibeasts

I can see a slug in the green grass.
I can smell a snail slithering and slithering
in the soil under the green grass.
I can feel a baby, little caterpillar crawling on my hands.
I can hear some butterflies flapping their wings
in the air.
I can taste sweetness in my lovely green garden.

Bella Mathieson (6)
Portsoy Primary School, Banff

Minibeasts

I can taste bees' honey and it is sweet.
I can see a spider's web dangling down from my roof.
I can hear worms turning the soil.
I can feel a snail's shell and it is rough.
I can smell bees' honey and it smells nice.

Olly McKenzie (6)
Portsoy Primary School, Banff

Minibeasts

I can see a ladybird crawling up my hand.
I can feel a slimy snail trail.
I can hear a bee buzzing up in the treetops.
I can taste the sweetness of the nectar.
I can smell some honey from the beehive.

Madison Taylor (7)
Portsoy Primary School, Banff

Untitled

I can see a snail that is slimy.
I can taste a snail.
I can feel an ant crawling up my arm.
I can smell some yummy honey.
I can hear a butterfly flapping its wings.

R-Jay Robertson (7)
Portsoy Primary School, Banff

Minibeasts

I can see a spider making a web.
I can taste gooey honey.
I can feel a sting of a bee.
I can smell dung from a dung beetle.
I can hear a beetle tapping its toes.

Oliver Merson (5)
Portsoy Primary School, Banff

Untitled

I can see a snail slithering along the ground.
I can taste sweet honey.
I can smell soil.
I can hear a bee buzzing.
I can feel a worm on my hand, it tickles.

Aidan Clark (6)
Portsoy Primary School, Banff

Nature

I can see a snail eating snail soup.
I can taste sticky honey.
I can feel a tickly beetle.
I can smell grass cuttings.
I can hear buzzing bees making honey.

Kenzi Gauld (6)
Portsoy Primary School, Banff

Minibeasts

I can see an orange ladybug with yellow spots.
I can hear a dragonfly.
I can taste honey from a hive.
I can smell a worm wriggling through the mud.

Mason John Taylor (7)
Portsoy Primary School, Banff

Minibeasts

I can see a stripy worm.
I can feel a lovely ladybird and a baby butterfly.
I can taste sticky yellow honey.
I can smell worms in rotting leaves.

Sienna Louise Angus (6)
Portsoy Primary School, Banff

Minibeasts

I can hear a butterfly flapping its wings.
I can feel a flower.
I can taste a flower's pollen.
I can smell the nice pollen from the flowers.

Ruby Rose Wilson (6)
Portsoy Primary School, Banff

Minibeasts

I can see a silky worm.
I can feel a baby butterfly on my finger.
I can smell a butterfly.
I can taste honey.

Alesha Wishart-Turner (6)
Portsoy Primary School, Banff

The Amazing Amazon

I can see a furry sloth in the dirty brown water.
I can smell chopped up wood and juicy lemons.
I can hear a loud growling jaguar and a squawking parrot.
I can feel sharp spiky wood and bumpy rough tree trunks.
I can taste a soft banana and cold fish.

Alfie David Goodwin (7)
Presteigne Primary School, Presteigne

The Amazing Amazon

I can see a monkey swinging in the trees.
I can smell a smelly crocodile in the water.
I can hear a snake hissing in the grass.
I can feel a jaguar in the grass.
I can taste a dust cloud in my mouth.

Mair Thomas (6)
Presteigne Primary School, Presteigne

The Amazing Amazon

I can feel a wet frog sitting on a rock.
I can smell the smelly bats.
I can hear slithering snakes.
I can see a slimy frog jumping on the logs.
I can taste a yellow banana.

John Andre Rodrigues-Nutting (7)
Presteigne Primary School, Presteigne

The Amazing Amazon

I can see a lazy sloth in the big tree.
I can smell a squashy banana on the damp floor.
I can hear a toucan squawking in the treetops.
I can feel a tiny tickly spider crawling up my arm.
I can taste salty rain falling from the dark sky
onto my tongue.

Benjamin Williams (7)
Presteigne Primary School, Presteigne

The Amazing Amazon

I can see a hairy monkey swinging from branch to branch.
I can smell a dirty monkey scratching his fleas.
I can hear a squawking parrot looking for his dad.
I can feel a hairy spider crawling up my arm.
I can taste a yucky squashed banana.

Ferdi Özsoylu (6)
Presteigne Primary School, Presteigne

The Amazing Amazon

I can see a slimy frog hopping through the grass.
I can smell some juicy mango soup in the trees.
I can hear a squawking parrot in the bright sky.
I can feel a scaly crocodile in the grass.
I can taste salty rain on my arm.

Chloe Lloyd-Bithell (7)
Presteigne Primary School, Presteigne

The Amazing Amazon

I can see a fluttering butterfly above the flowers.
I can smell a sweet flower amongst the long grass.
I can hear a squawking macaw sitting on a branch.
I can feel a feathery bird when I touch it with my arm.
I can taste a sweet, juicy orange.

Darcy Barden (7)
Presteigne Primary School, Presteigne

The Amazing Amazon

I can see a parrot squawking to find its food.
I can smell a stinky rat.
I can hear a jaguar searching for its food.
I can feel swishing water.
I can taste a wet mango fallen from the tree.

Hunter Jones (6)
Presteigne Primary School, Presteigne

The Amazing Amazon

I can see crawling ants carrying leaves.
I can smell a smelly sloth.
I can hear a squawking parrot looking for his mummy.
I can feel raindrops dripping on my hand.
I can taste a sweet mango.

Finley James Williams (6)
Presteigne Primary School, Presteigne

The Amazing Amazon

I can see a slithery snake in the tree.
I can smell the stinky bats flapping around the trees
I can hear a cheeky monkey chatting.
I can taste the salty rain.
I can feel a spider on my arm.

Katie Mae Williams (6)
Presteigne Primary School, Presteigne

The Amazing Amazon

I can see a jumping tree frog.
I can smell fresh flowers growing.
I can hear a jaguar hunting down its prey.
I can feel tiny ants hitting me.
I can taste the dust as it blows towards me.

Rhys Morgan (7)
Presteigne Primary School, Presteigne

The Amazing Amazon

I can see a bright bird flying in the sky.
I can smell sweet flowers.
I can hear a slimy snake slithering through the grass.
I can feel a tiny ant on my hand.
I can taste a soft banana.

Max Scott (6)
Presteigne Primary School, Presteigne

The Amazing Amazon

I can see a tiger hunting for his dinner.
I can smell the beautiful flowers.
I can hear the flowing river.
I can feel a hairy sloth.
I can taste the delicious bananas.

Josie Simcock (7)
Presteigne Primary School, Presteigne

Summer Poem

I hear birds chirping, trees blowing,
Bees buzzing, an ice cream van singing.
I taste ice cream, cold drinks with ice,
Ice lollies and burgers on the barbecue.
I smell cut grass, tall trees, suncream,
Gorgeous flowers, and the barbecue.
I see butterflies, lovely flowers, grass,
The sun and tall trees.
I touch beautiful flowers, grass and my house.

Lauren Martin (7)
St Charles Primary School, Glasgow

A Lovely Summer's Day

I hear lovely bees buzzing away
on a summer's day.
I taste lovely and brilliant chocolate ice cream
on a summer's day.
I touch colourful flowers
on a bright summer's day.
I see lovely bunnies on a lovely summer's day
in the green grass.

Ruby Cosh
St Charles Primary School, Glasgow

The Rainforest

The rainforest looks like animals like cheetahs.
The rainforest tastes like munchy chewy bananas.
It has bears and butterflies.
You can see monkeys eating crunchy bananas
as they climb up the trees.
You can eat mangoes and juicy oranges.
It feels like a jungle.

Luke Bierey (7)
St Charles Primary School, Glasgow

The Beach

I hear birds tweeting.
I taste yummy hot dogs.
I can touch wet seashells.
I can smell salty seaweed.
I can hear waves crash.

Ellie Joanna Joanna Drysdale (5)
St Charles Primary School, Glasgow

The Rainforest

The rainforest looks like yellow cheetahs.
The rainforest tastes like munchy chewy bananas.
The rainforest looks like monkeys climbing.
The rainforest tastes like mangoes.
The rainforest smells like a sloth and hot rain.
The rainforest smells like sweet flowers.

Ayat Amin (7)
St Charles Primary School, Glasgow

Summer Poem

I hear beautiful lawnmowers cutting the lovely grass.
I taste the barbecue, it is lovely.
I smell the lovely butterflies eating nectar.
I touch the lovely grass and flowers and the gorgeous plants.
I see all the cars and trucks driven in the lovely sun.

Cerys Anne Newman (7)
St Charles Primary School, Glasgow

Rainforest Senses

I can see the animals fighting over the food.
I can hear the monkeys fighting over the bananas.
I can taste the fruits growing on the trees.
I can smell the lovely wildflowers.
I can touch a slimy snake's skin.

Charley Helen McEwan (7)
St Charles Primary School, Glasgow

The Rainforest

The rainforest looks like a big green snake.
The rainforest smells like a big cat.
The rainforest feels like snakes.
The rainforest sounds like chattering chimps.
The rainforest tastes like munchy, chewy bananas.

Jack James McGonigle (7)
St Charles Primary School, Glasgow

Summer's Day

I hear the ice cream van out the front.
I taste yummy slush puppies.
I smell a barbecue in my friend's garden.
I touch the cold water at my swimming pool.
I see beautiful butterflies.

Aliex Murray (7)
St Charles Primary School, Glasgow

Springtime

I hear the beautiful birds.
I taste strawberry and Nutella, yum-yum.
I smell ice cream, chocolate and Milky Way bars.
I touch little dogs and beautiful flowers.
I see pretty flowers in the soothing grass.

Beth Wilson (7)
St Charles Primary School, Glasgow

Summer Poem

I hear bees buzzing around me.
I taste yummy ice cream from an ice cream truck.
I smell burgers from the barbecue.
I see the nice sun.
I touch the soft fur on my cat.

Emily Tollett (7)
St Charles Primary School, Glasgow

The Beach

I see sparkly shells.
I hear waves crashing.
I smell fish and chips.
I taste cold ice cream.
I feel the hot sand.

Ayaan Azam (6)
St Charles Primary School, Glasgow

The Beach

I hear birds tweeting.
I taste yummy hot dogs.
I can touch wet seashells.
I can smell salty seaweed.
I can see the fish in the sea.

Grace Olivia Anderson (5)
St Charles Primary School, Glasgow

Beach

I hear birds sing.
I taste yummy hot dogs.
I can touch warm sand.
I can smell salty seaweed.
I can see fish in the sea.

Shay Farquhar (5)
St Charles Primary School, Glasgow

The Beach

I hear people laughing.
I taste yummy hot dogs.
I can touch wet seashells.
I can smell salty seaweed.
I can see fish in the sea.

Olivia Teresa Dougan-Wark
St Charles Primary School, Glasgow

The Beach

I see the glittery sand.
I hear seagulls squawking.
I smell the salty sea.
I taste fish and chips.
I feel the hot sun.

Lewis Hamilton (5)
St Charles Primary School, Glasgow

The Beach

I hear birds tweeting.
I taste yummy hot dogs.
I can touch the wet sea.
I can smell salty seaweed.
I can see waves crashing.

Daniel McGhee (5)
St Charles Primary School, Glasgow

The Beach

I hear people laughing.
I taste cold ice cream.
I can touch warm sand.
I can smell salty seaweed.
I can see fish in the sea.

Olivia Grace Bradley (5)
St Charles Primary School, Glasgow

The Beach

I hear people laughing.
I taste cold ice cream.
I can touch warm sand.
I can smell salty seaweed.
I can see fish in the sea.

Ryan James O'Hara (5)
St Charles Primary School, Glasgow

The Beach

I see the sparkly sea.
I hear waves crashing.
I smell fish and chips.
I taste the fish and chips.
I feel the hot sand.

Rayyan Amin (5)
St Charles Primary School, Glasgow

The Beach

I hear people laughing
I taste cold ice cream
I can touch wet seashells
I can smell seaweed
I can see waves crashing.

Charlotte Kelly (6)
St Charles Primary School, Glasgow

The Beach

I see bright yellow sand
I hear seagulls squawking
I smell fish and chips
I taste cold ice cream
I feel the hot sand.

Taylor Bokas (5)
St Charles Primary School, Glasgow

The Beach

I see sparkly seashells.
I hear waves crashing.
I smell fish and chips.
I taste fish and chips.
I feel the hot sun.

Shay Arkinson (5)
St Charles Primary School, Glasgow

Untitled

I see sparkly seashells.
I hear children squealing.
I smell yummy food.
I taste cold ice cream
I feel cold water.

Brody Boyd (5)
St Charles Primary School, Glasgow

The Beach

I can see a fish.
I hear waves crashing.
I smell the salty sea.
I taste fish and chips.
I feel the hot sun.

Connor Craig (5)
St Charles Primary School, Glasgow

The Beach

I see sparkly seashells.
I hear seagulls squawk.
I smell food.
I taste cold ice cream.
I feel the cold sea.

Abigail Kirkland (6)
St Charles Primary School, Glasgow

The Beach

I see sparkly shells.
I hear waves.
I smell yummy food.
I taste cold ice cream.
I feel happy.

Keira Faith McDonald (6)
St Charles Primary School, Glasgow

Summer Poem

I hear beautiful birds tweeting and cars.
I taste brilliant ice creams and sausages.
I touch colourful flowers and trees.
I see a lovely blue sky and the sun.

Katrine Friel (7)
St Charles Primary School, Glasgow

The Rain

Rain sounds like *drip-drop* on the house
Rain feels tickly
Rain helps you to see things better
Rain smells like grass
Rain tastes like broccoli pasta.

Lily May (5)
Straiton Primary School, Maybole

Young Writers Information

We hope you have enjoyed reading this book – and that you will continue to in the coming years.

If you're a young writer who enjoys reading and creative writing, or the parent of an enthusiastic poet or story writer, do visit our website www.youngwriters.co.uk. Here you will find free competitions, workshops and games, as well as recommended reads, a poetry glossary and our blog.

If you would like to order further copies of this book, or any of our other titles give us a call or visit www.youngwriters.co.uk.

Young Writers
Remus House
Coltsfoot Drive
Peterborough
PE2 9BF

(01733) 890066
info@youngwriters.co.uk

Share your feelings verse any time!